Freya

BY VIRGINIA LOH-HAGAN

Gods and goddesses were the main characters of myths. Myths are traditional stories from ancient cultures. Storytellers answered questions about the world by creating exciting explanations. People thought myths were true. Myths explained the unexplainable. They helped people make sense of human behavior and nature. Today, we use science to explain the world. But people still love myths. Myths may not be literally true. But they have meaning. They tell us something about our history and culture.

45th Parallel Press

Published in the United States of America by Cherry Lake Publishing
Ann Arbor, Michigan
www.cherrylakepublishing.com

Content Adviser: Alexandra Krasowski, Worcester Art Museum, Harvard University (Extension School)
Reading Adviser: Marla Conn MS, Ed., Literacy specialist, Read-Ability, Inc.
Book Design: Jen Wahi

Photo Credits: © Gino Santa Maria/Shutterstock.com, 5; © Skylines/Shutterstock.com, 6; © Radharani/Shutterstock.com, 8; © archetype/Shutterstock.com, 11; © Yasmins world/Shutterstock.com, 13; © Tereshchenko Dmitry/Shutterstock.com, 15; © GlebSStock/Shutterstock.com, 17; © Susanitah/Shutterstock.com, 19; © aSuruwataRi/Shutterstock.com, 21; © Homo Cosmicos/Shutterstock.com, 22; © Soare Cecilia Corina/Shutterstock.com, 27; © coka/Shutterstock.com, 29; © Howard David Johnson, 2018, Cover, 1, 25; Various art elements throughout, Shutterstock.com

45th Parallel Press is an imprint of Cherry Lake Publishing.

Library of Congress Cataloging-in-Publication Data

Names: Loh-Hagan, Virginia, author.
Title: Freya / by Virginia Loh-Hagan.
Description: Ann Arbor : Cherry Lake Publishing, 2018. | Series: Gods and goddesses of the ancient world |
    Includes bibliographical references and index.
Identifiers: LCCN 2018003332 | ISBN 9781534129429 (hardcover) | ISBN 9781534131125 (pdf) |
    ISBN 9781534132627 (pbk.) | ISBN 9781534134324 (hosted ebook)
Subjects: LCSH: Freya (Norse deity)—Juvenile literature.
Classification: LCC BL870.F48 L64 2018 | DDC 293/.2114—dc23
LC record available at https://lccn.loc.gov/2018003332

Printed in the United States of America
Corporate Graphics

ABOUT THE AUTHOR:

Dr. Virginia Loh-Hagan is an author, university professor, former classroom teacher, and curriculum designer. Books and movies make her cry very easily. Too bad her tears aren't jewels. She lives in San Diego with her very tall husband and very naughty dogs. To learn more about her, visit www.virginialoh.com.

TABLE OF CONTENTS

CHAPTER 1

HOSTAGES

Who is Freya? What happened between the Aesir and Vanir?

Freya was a **Norse** goddess. Norse means from the Norway area. She was the goddess of love. She was the goddess of beauty. She was the goddess of war. She was the goddess of death. She was the goddess of **fertility**. Fertility is the ability to make babies. Many women prayed to her. They wanted help with childbirth. They wanted help with marriage. They wanted to have good crops.

Freya was really beautiful. She had blonde hair. She had blue eyes. She was called "the **Fair** One." Fair means pretty. Every woman wanted to be Freya. Every man wanted to marry her.

There were two tribes of Norse gods and goddesses. They were the Vanir and the Aesir. Freya was a Vanir goddess.

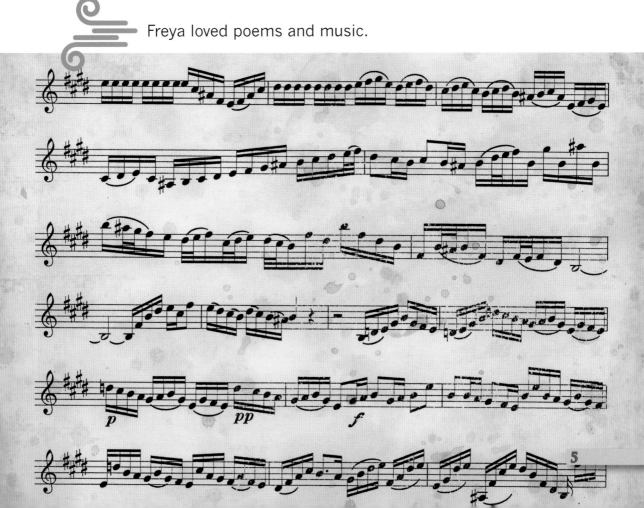

Freya loved poems and music.

Most of the stories we know are about the Aesir tribe.

She practiced magic. She could control fate. She sat on a high throne. She wore animal skins. She wore gloves made from cats' skins. To see things, she ate animal hearts.

She moved from town to town. She sold her magic. She went to **Asgard**. Asgard was at the universe's center. It was heaven. It was where the Aesir lived.

The Aesir fell in love with Freya. They wanted her magic. But some Aesir gods and goddesses became mad. They believed in honor, loyalty, and law. Freya's magic upset their beliefs.

Family Tree

Grandparent: Buri (god of creation)

Parents: Njord (god of sea, wind, and storm), Nerthus (Mother Earth)

Brother: Freyr (god of good fortune, sunshine, and fair weather)

Spouse: Odr (symbol of the summer sun)

Children: Hnoss (goddess of desire and lust), Gersemi (goddess of beauty and possessions)

The Aesir blamed Freya. The Aesir tried to kill her. They burned her three times. But Freya wouldn't die. She rose from the ashes.

This soured relations between the Aesir and Vanir. They didn't trust each other. They went to war. The Aesir fought with weapons and force. The Vanir fought with magic. The war lasted for years.

They finally got tired of fighting. They made a peace deal. They traded **hostages**. Hostages are like prisoners. Freya, her **twin** brother, and her father were sent to the Aesir. Twins are siblings born at the same time. Two Aesir gods were sent to the Vanir. The Vanir hostages were treated well. The Aesir hostages were not.

The Aesir called Freya "Gullveig." This means "greedy for gold."

CHAPTER 2

FAMILY COMES FIRST

Who is Odr? What are "Freya's tears"? Who are Freya's daughters?

Freya married Odr. Odr was a god. He was not as famous as Freya. He liked being unknown. He liked not being recognized. It meant nobody bothered him. He was a symbol of the summer sun. Like the sun, he went everywhere. He liked to travel. He would go away for a long time. He gained wisdom from the world. He would leave Freya by herself.

Freya loved Odr a lot. She missed him when he was gone. She followed him. She traveled around the world. She tried to find him. She disguised herself. She used different names.

She was sad. She cried. Some of her tears fell to the ground. They turned into gold. Gold was called "Freya's tears." Some of her tears fell into the sea. These turned into **amber**. Amber is tree gum that has turned to rock.

Freya and Odr had two daughters. They were Hnoss and Gersemi. They were beautiful like Freya. They were charming like Odr. They missed their parents when they were away.

Vikings, or Norse people, respected those who traveled a lot.

All in the Family

Freyr was Freya's twin brother. He was the god of good fortune. He was the god of sunshine. He was the god of fair weather. He was the god of fertility. Some Swedish kings and queens might be related to him. He was beautiful. He had muscles. He had long, flowing hair. He was the lord of the elves. He had a magical boar. He had a magical chariot. The chariot was pulled by boars. Freyr brought peace wherever the chariot went. Freyr also had a magical ship. The ship always sailed in good wind. It could be folded together. It could be carried in a pocket. Freyr fell in love with a giant. Her name was Gerd. Gerd didn't love Freyr back. Freyr asked his servant Skirnir to help him. Freyr had a magical sword. He would die without the sword. Freyr lent the sword to Skirnir. He wanted Skirnir to use it to bring Gerd to him. Freyr traded the sword for Gerd. He was willing to die for love.

Freya's daughters' names mean "jewels."

There are a few stories about Odr not coming back. Freya found out what happened. Odr was lost at sea. He disobeyed orders. The Aesir punished him. They turned Odr into a sea monster. Odr was killed. Freya killed the man who killed Odr.

CHAPTER 3

WOMAN WARRIOR

How does Freya support war? What does she do for the underworld?

Vikings were Norse people. They were explorers. They were **warriors**. Warriors are fighters. They sailed to different places. They raided towns. They attacked people. They had a warrior culture. They raised their children to fight. They trained to fight. They knew people died in war. So, they had lots of children. They wanted more warriors. That's why Freya was important. She made people fertile. She helped people have babies.

Fertility was in Freya's blood. Her father was a god of the sea. Her mother was Mother Earth. Her twin brother was a sun

god. They all brought life to the world. They provided food.
They made animals. They made plants. They fed warriors.

Twins are a sign of fertility.

Freya was the goddess of war and death. She was in charge of Folkvang. It was a warrior's field. Her castle was called Sessrumnir. This means "room of seats." It was part of the **underworld**. The underworld is where dead people go. She took the souls of dead war heroes. She split half with Odin. Odin was the father of the gods. He lived in **Valhalla**. This means "hall of the dead."

Odin ruled the **Valkyries**. Valkyries were female spirits. They were dark angels of death. They were warrior women. They flew over battlefields. They took the strong warriors. They took the war heroes.

Some went to Freya in Sessrumnir. Others went to Odin in Valhalla. There were plenty of seats for dead souls in Sessrumnir. Freya fed them. She took care of them. She built their strength. She needed their help to rebuild the world.

 Some people think the Valkyries were the daughters of Freya and Odin.

Real World Connection

Like Freya, Lynea Lattanzio loves cats. She's over 60 years old. She got a divorce. She was sad. She sold her car. She sold her diamond ring. She started caring for cats. She's rescued over 1,000 cats. The cats live in her 4,200-square-foot (390-square-meters) house. Lattanzio lives in a trailer by her house. She doesn't have any cages. She doesn't kill any cats. Her house is called Cat House on the Kings. It's in California. It's the biggest cat shelter. Lattanzio protects wild and lost cats. (She even has some peacocks.) She became a vet technician to keep medical costs low. She began taking care of cats in 1992. She said, "I'm at the top of the list of eccentric cat ladies. I don't think there has been anyone who has lived with 28,000 cats in 24 years."

Not much is known about Sessrumnir.

Freya had a deal with Odin. She got first pick of the dead warriors. The Valkyries took the dead to Freya's home. She picked which warriors she wanted. She had them stay with her. The other warriors went to Odin's home.

Freya also opened up her underworld to women. She took in women who died **noble** deaths. Noble means honorable. Freya greeted these women who died.

CHAPTER 4

CATS, PIGS, AND FALCONS— OH MY!

How does Freya travel? What are her symbols?

Freya was often seen riding her **chariot**. Chariots are carts with two wheels. They're pulled by animals. Freya's chariot was pulled by two cats. Her cats were big. They were male. They were blue.

There is a story about how Thor gave Freya her cats. Thor is the god of thunder. Thor was fishing. He heard beautiful singing. Bayun was a magical male cat. He was singing to his two blue kittens. Bayun asked Thor for help. Thor took the kittens. He gave them to Freya. Then Bayun turned into a bird. He flew away.

Freya also had a magical pig. Pigs are symbols of wealth and fertility. The pig's name was Hildisvini. It means "battle pig." It was made by **dwarfs**. Dwarfs were magical creatures that lived in mines. When she didn't ride the chariot, Freya rode the pig. The pig had golden **bristles**. Bristles are hair. The bristles glowed. They helped Freya see in the dark.

Cats have symbolized women since ancient Egypt.

Ottar built a temple for Freya.

Some stories say the pig was Ottar. Ottar was Freya's human love. Freya turned Ottar into a pig. Freya rode the pig. They searched for his family. They met a witch. The witch told Ottar about his family.

Freya had a magical **cloak**. Cloaks are like capes. Freya's cloak was made of **falcon** feathers. Falcons are birds of prey. They hunt. They have great eyesight. They are strong flyers.

Cross-Cultural Connection

Ixchel was an ancient Mayan goddess. Like Freya, she was the goddess of many things. She was the goddess of the moon. She was the goddess of love. She was a war goddess. She was the goddess of childbirth. She was the goddess of medicine. She helped women give birth. She helped women heal. She married the sun god. She had 13 children. She always had a rabbit with her. She had jaguar claws. She had jaguar ears. She wore a snake on her head. The snake was like a crown. Ixchel had crossbones on her skirt. Mayan women worshiped her. They formed a community. They made a temple for her. They lived on an island. The island is called Isla Mujeres. This means "Island of Women." It's off the coast of Cancún. Women went to the temple. They prayed for sons.

Freya wore her cloak. She became a falcon. She could fly. She could travel anywhere she wanted. She could travel to different worlds. She could travel quickly. She liked flying at night. She flew over people's homes. She helped people fall in love.

Many gods wanted her cloak. They borrowed it. Thor borrowed the cloak. His hammer was stolen. The cloak helped him get his hammer back.

 Being able to fly is a powerful skill.

CHAPTER 5

BEAUTIFUL FREYA

What are some stories about Freya? What happened with the walls of Asgard? What is Brisingamen?

There are many myths about Freya.

This myth is about Freya and the walls of Asgard. Giants attacked Asgard. Walls were built to keep giants away. A builder was hired. He wanted to marry Freya. The gods promised Freya to him. But the builder had to build the walls in a year and a day. The gods didn't think he could do it. But the builder had a magical horse. The horse did twice as much work as a man. The builder was going to win. The gods tricked the builder. A god changed into a female horse. He lured the magical horse away. The builder was mad. Thor killed him.

Freya had a famous necklace. Its name was Brisingamen. This means "jewelry of fire."

There were four dwarfs. They made the most beautiful necklace. Freya wanted it. She tried to pay them with gold. But the dwarfs didn't want gold. They each wanted to marry Freya for a day. She agreed. After four nights, she got the necklace.

Freya was often the object of desire.

Loki is a trickster god. He turned into a flea. He stole her necklace. He agreed to give it back if Freya started a war.

Explained By Science

People cry. Tears come out of people's eyes. Tears are a mix of water, protein, mucus, and oil. There are three different types of tears. First, there are basal tears. Basal tears are always in eyes. They keep eyes from drying out. Some may come out through the nose. This causes runny noses. Second, there are reflex tears. These tears are mostly water. They keep out things like smoke, dust, or onion fumes. Eye nerves tell the brain to cry. Reflex tears get rid of bad stuff. They protect eyes. Third, there are emotional tears. These tears respond to feelings. The brain feels sadness or happiness. This releases hormones in eyes. Then tears form. Crying lets go of poison from the bodies. People feel better after crying. Humans are the only living things that cry emotional tears. Animals cry in fear or need. But they don't make tears.

Freya was sad about her husband. Beautiful things made her feel better.

Freya did. She made two kings fight. She used her magic. She made the dead come alive again. Warriors kept fighting. The war never ended.

Don't anger the goddesses. Freya had great powers. And she knew how to use them.

DID YOU KNOW?

- Freya means "lady." Her twin brother was Freyr. That means "lord."

- Freyasdaeg is Friday. It was probably named after her or Frigg. Frigg was Odin's wife.

- Freya is also known as Vanadis. This means "lady of the Vanir." Vanadium is an element. It's named after her.

- Freya is also known as Gefn. Gefn means "giver."

- During the Viking Age, husbands went to war. Wives were upset. They were worried. Freya represents these Norse wives.

- Freya's name is used in other words. For example, noble Norse women are called fru. Another example comes from Germany. Frau is a German word. It means "woman."

- Farmers plant crops. They say her name. This promises them a good harvest.

- Sometimes, Freya is confused with Frigg. But Frigg was an Aesir. And Freya was a Vanir.

- Another name for Freya is Horn. This is related to the word for flax, "horr." Bundles of flax have been found at Freya's worship sites. Sacrificed animals, weapons, and gold rings have also been found at her sites. People give these things in hopes of getting rich.

- Freya was still worshiped after people converted to Christianity.

- Three giants wanted to marry Freya. But Thor killed them.

- Freya embodies the "volva." This is a person who practices "seidr." Seidr is the most organized form of ancient Norse magic.

- Freya is connected to spring. Freyr is connected to fall. Freya inspires seeds to grow. Freyr helps harvest crops. They work together.

CONSIDER THIS!

TAKE A POSITION! Freya has many jobs. What are they? Which one do you think is most important? Argue your point with reasons and evidence.

SAY WHAT? Read the 45th Parallel Press book about Frigg. Compare Freya and Frigg. Explain how they're the same. Explain how they're different.

THINK ABOUT IT! Freya loved beautiful things. Beautiful things made her feel better. Make a list of things that you think are beautiful. Make a list of things that make you feel better.

LEARN MORE

Long, Christopher E., and Mike Dubisch (illus.). *Freya.* Edina, MN: Magic Wagon, 2011.

Napoli, Donna Jo, and Christina Balit (illus.). *Treasury of Norse Mythology: Stories of Intrigue, Trickery, Love, and Revenge.* Washington, DC: National Geographic, 2015.

GLOSSARY

amber (AM-ber) tree gum that has turned to rock

Asgard (AHS-gahrd) center of the universe where the Aesir Norse gods lived

bristles (BRIS-uhlz) tough hair

chariot (CHAR-ee-uht) two-wheeled cart pulled by animals

cloak (KLOHK) cape or coat

dwarfs (DWORFZ) magical creatures who mine and make magical weapons

fair (FARE) beautiful

falcon (FAWL-kuhn) bird of prey

fertility (fer-TIL-ih-tee) the ability to make babies

hostages (HOS-tij-iz) prisoners taken for a reason

noble (NOH-buhl) honorable

Norse (NORS) coming from the Norway area

twin (TWIN) one of two children born at the same time from the same mother

underworld (UHN-dur-wurld) the place where the souls of dead people go after they die

Valhalla (val-HAL-uh) hall of the dead where killed warriors are welcomed

Valkyries (val-KEER-eez) female warrior spirits who fly over battlefields and take fallen war heroes to Freya's or Odin's hall

Vikings (VYE-kingz) seafaring warriors who raided and attacked towns

warriors (WAWR-ee-erz) fighters

INDEX